I0807314

What Happens At Canals

Sam DiFalco

What Happens At Canals

The Mansfield Press

Canadian Cataloguing in Publication Data

Difalco, Sam
What Happens At Canals

Poems
ISBN 1-894469-06-2

1. Title
PS8557.I397W4 2001 C811'.6 C2001-901883-5
PR9199.4.D54W4 2001

Acknowledgements:

Antigonish Review
Ariel
Caliban
Dandelion
Exquisite Corpse
The Fiddlehead
Malahat Review
Matrix
Paperplates
Poetry Canada Review
Poet's Gallery
Prairie Fire
Scrivener
TickleAce
Toronto Life
Wascana Review
Windsor Review

Cover and text design by Darren Holmes
Author photo on page 48 by Bruno Crescia
Cover photo by D. Falconer

The publication of *What Happens At Canals* has been generously supported by The Canada Council for the Arts.

The Canada Council for the Arts
Le Conseil des Arts du Canada

Mansfield Press Inc.
25 Mansfield Avenue, Toronto, Ontario, Canada, M6J 2A9
Publisher: Denis De Klerck

for Alexandra

Contents

What Happens At Canals

First Poke Your Eyes

There are milder things in the envelope.
Given that pain is lending an ear and finding the
proceedings dull. The needles are white and breathless,
a soft red fuzz drifts to and from the yellow blurs
of hidden movement, too fine for human optic nerves.

And in the green gas surrounding the birth
of effortless being, the eyes are bathed
at first glance, and then reduced to pinpricks.

Amenities

Bettina sits me to tea
sets a pale yellow pot
down on a teal blue table

surrounds it with matching
cups creamer sugar bowl
laughs at the large

porcelain flower she
has arranged between us.
The tea steeps too long

as she goes on about
how symmetry and
order are beautiful

necessary even in
the most mundane
things. Pours it like

black perfume into
my cup and politely
I pretend to sip

as she tells me sadly
that the last batch
she brewed

withered some pretty
jonquils she was growing
out back by the pool.

Dragon

Something isn't right
a weightlessness a small
disturbance in the lighting.

Butterflies batter paper walls
suffering dreams
hallucinations.

The greenskinned lady whispering
Nothing is perfect nothing
is perfect.

Late Of April

I thought she would bring me green
helmets and warm velvet breezes.
My frostbitten valley was due.

I've pined for her vague violins,
for her flutes and hints of
blue piano (she can improvise).

But the genius is still asleep,
bleak notions fester unabated
under my heavy, rooty duvet.

The slush appalls me, grinds me down,
no sun shines on my endless days.
Blah incarnate, pasty, limp,

I have no will to lift myself. My music
is a drum of frozen cattle lard
struck dully with a moose's antler.

I cannot partake of the beautiful
things in my life, the liberty,
the pageantry, the excess.

Nor do I desire
a lusty frog-jump into summer.
All I want is only what is Spring.

Lunch On The Green

Buttercups and poppies make us sneeze
as we proceed from path to garden party.
You unyoke your raw silk dress like a sun
upon the grass near the almond tree
and a fragrant afternoon takes shape.

The maidens will refrain from faltering now
though their smooth legs shimmer under swirls.
And nodding chaps in black patent pumps
will kick up sod and strike their sticks
then cry, Well here we are and how about that!

And with indiscretions intimated only by
a lowering of the left eye or a sidelong cast
from a hat of immaculate felt
who knows when lunch will end!

The tree offers ballast in the blazing green
and flaccid you snooze at the core of the scene.

Bal Masqué

One finds it all a little swarming
for a late midsummer afternoon:
the teeming hats and hubbub and hucksters
blowing tin-horns at the harlequins,
hoarse-throated huhs and hums
and laughter from the wolfish scrum
overwhelming the sweetmeat table.

In this garden extravaganza
one declines to draw conclusions;
the eyes under the domino are better
left unopen, unable to digest
the buggy light and vegetation,
restless forms and motivations
put in motion when the day winds down.

And when the day winds down the moon arrives,
the garden lamps flare on, and suddenly
the scene is jewelled teeth and bayonets,
crinoline and pompadours,
spitted suckling pig and rum
and wolf-fur under the leafy shrubs
behind the convulsive orchestra . . .

The eyes go up, the mind bends over.
And a boozy bulk of sighs and screams
assaults the evening proper.

Sottostare

Imagine that your life is going on
in the other half of the room.
The woman behind the curtains
studies you for a time before
she gestures to the little dog
who silently responds, eyes moist,
tiny tail unbending . . .

Others carry on the card game,
pausing to fill the air with smoke or foul replies,
glancing at their pocketwatches
or at the paper clock above your head.

They are familiar to you, though you yourself
lack substance, one side of you in shadow
the other self-absorbed in shirt-sleeves.
Yet someone like yourself is
winking at them, winking at you,
lingering over the curtain's rich brocade,
whistling underbreath for the dog . . .

Or is some further strangeness represented,
the truth of you behind the smile?
Your last joke pleased everyone,
their easygoing silence brims with praise.
But you purposely never complete
the sentence that would please them further.

Rosalia

Somewhere in Tuscany
monks flex their throats
but I hear the pauses
in nondescript jazz tunes.

A woman with a husky voice
told me distance dulls the heart.
Where was I then? She was fried
on the acid everyone had taken
after singing me Happy Birthday.

Made it out finally
or at least most of me.
My friend over there
likes Gregorian chants.
Called her this morning.
She wasn't home
her segreteria telefonica
on the blink.

I accelerate up the road
toward the dark green escarpment.

Where am I going again?
Up the road
toward the dark green escarpment.

Home Dream

We sat naked
in the kitchen eating bread
and drinking milk
before our bedtime
but come morning
simple fruit filled the bowl
with the light dripping
from above—the way
I left them sitting there
waving into the stream
and lifting their hot eyes
as in dreams when one smiles
and the smile doubles everything.

What Happens At Canals

Everyone takes their shoes off
down by the canal.

Even Max the old sailor
fishing from the dock
red hat
green anchor tattoo.
Beside him: red deck shoes
with yellow socks neatly folded on top.

Men in dull flannels
floating through the powderblue water
must not have their shoes on (they may be
the small slate lumps on the other side of the canal).

And ladies in floral dresses
men and children in crayons
lunch lightly on cream tablecloths
unfurled upon the grass (indeed quite green).
They too have removed their shoes
and have rested them sparkling black by the dock.
They were not wearing socks it seems.

(But it isn't warm enough or really
proper for these people to disrobe
further—so they will not.)

The man in the green fibreglass boat
in the middle of the canal has let his oars go slack
and has wiped his brow with a black handkerchief.
He is unlacing his unseen shoes now too.

Picasso Negro

To leap upon a thin horse and ride away:
or this fist that gathers darkness
there, in rooms of whitest taffeta and lace.
She lacks a blue bull and his familiar horns
under the virginal canopy,
his fervent breath, his sperm.

Beside the painted faces on the wall,
his many-fingered hands massage her carnal soles,
remove her old spun copper dressings.
Only then will she suspend
her attachment to the dream.
Her hands will find the black guitar
and she will play again.

Christmas Song

They will help with the tree,
the mourners, they will make it lovely.

The dolls, too, lovely.
The one in black puts on the hats.

All of them in black, the one
with black hair, no hands.

I knew her in another life.
I was standing by a lake

in another life and she was
combing the shallows for hands.

"I will fish your heart too, don't laugh."
But mine was soft.

There, in the blue fog,
searching for gestures she never had.

Waiting

Pretending to read in green light
with a false look of intensity
—the trembling sweeping hands
of the clock have never been slower.

Outside a monster gnashes his teeth
in the boreal roar, the skirmishes
of ruthless winds not pretty, not
the breezes of beautiful legends.

The fireside fairy-tales sputter.
The house is old it's true and
as a consequence is colder too.
Friendly waves do nothing for

my fingers finding shelter under
anything that's friendly. One, two,
both hands bearded now, I am unable
to move. Except for the shivering.

Shivering to death while reading
of the fireplace, and intimate
winters. Yes, there is sleep to consider,
and dreams, but mainly there is waiting.

What You Need To Know

The reins aren't there for you
to yank on. Hock boots shield

the cannon bones on jumps;
numnah spares the back from galls.

Compare the spinal column to a bridge.
No complaints about the swaying yet.

Pull lightly on the reins.
Milk teeth yield to permanents, like yours.

Titbits go a long way in the fetching field
and in a pinch sugar lumps will do.

Motor of the pony:
stifles, hocks, and gaskins.

The hoof grows out of the coronet.
Frogs absorb the shock.

Remember that the snaffle rubs a delicate part
of the mouth.

Pull lightly on the reins
or he will run away.

Fire Plum

Strip birch for shelter.
Light fire—pray
at moon rise

—meshes shine with fish

black canoes slide by —

Ask Him many questions.
He will seem a shadow in the open.

All the time you pass in sleep is yours.
"I am lost."
I am lost.

Ill-Advised God

He's listening,
ear pressed against the rough red brick.
He fills up the space in my absence.
Sometimes I hear Him whispering.

It's not true of course.
He's not true, nor am I.

Predomination At The Quarry

My russet pug concerns itself
with something unseen across the man-made lake.
A breeze explains the slight.

Sailing crafts slide by the dam
uneasy platinum on calamine blue.
And generators billow chrysotile.

Belly-deep the bathers wade
shivering sallow-breasted, gingerly plopping,
khaki caps pulled tight.

The watchers fully clothed in linen suits
sigh deeply on the lawn's crushed green
and at my cuffs a rough snore steams a stain.

The sun is relentless
though the bathers brace themselves and mist the air
and others breathe palms warm.

We shall not stay for long with cobalt clouds nearby,
we know enough to leave this place.
The faces of our silent friends grow pale.

Across the man-made lake
the dainty waders are withdrawing to the shore.
The humming dam has paused.

Where have the scudding vessels gone? Where are they
now? They have fled without goodbyes.
And shall we flee quite soon, before the bathers dry?

Asylum

I am a little weary at this other extreme, lurking in the foliage.
The small green raft drifts away from me now,
down a channel of broken chalices—the river as dreamed,
the mast tipping slowly into the mist
as we dreamt it would. Yellow pollen,
blackgreen leaves: if the tree warrants any submissions
nothing I can say will change the course of things.
The truth is not quite visible beneath the shredded veils
though I try to perceive, clinging to chimeras
like children I have lost . . .

You could see me from the other side,
in the schoolchalk structure, its sombre square eyes
mediating our fractured
communion: and the river tinkled on
without ceremony, liquefying only as the sun set.

A Poetics of Rain

The sky was raining scorpions and eels
I hid in a doorway and waited.
Quite a mess we had on our hands
all manner of siren-blaring
citizens vomiting in the streets.
We had no stomach for
this sort of storm.

The sky darkened again and bloodless children's feet
came down toes wriggling.
We gathered the feet
lacquered the tiny toenails
and paraded them in public to applause.

Then hands fell from the sky
dark hands with long fingers and pale
palms falling in pairs
conducting invisible orchestras
alarming our sensibilities.
We loaded the hands on boats
transported them to island prisons off the coast.

It's raining again.
Now poets fall from the skies
well-fed poets with feathery tongues flicking
in and out of their mouths
poets plump in the ankles and wrists
poets wearing scarewigs
poets with no hands and no feet.

Indeed they frighten us
and we herd them after the rains
but don't know what to do with them
maybe send them back to the sky
and fearing a monsoon
we are debating whether to build
domes over our cities.

Untitled #9

The glass crackles in her hand
red wine spills on the sheets and then
blood and she sits naked in the bed
smiling her eyes looking through me.

I occupy the chair disquieted by
my detachment more than the bright stain
spreading around her as she holds
the hand between her thighs.

We make love immediately
cutting ourselves on the shards.

In the morning we will hang out the sheet
let it dry then promptly deliver it
to a gallery that's been
favourable to our work of late.

Less Pleasant Music

Kiss me and watch a patient hand
caress the other, less innocent insinuations:
the snake in the grass, smiling at his
smallness, at his anonymity.
And yet how gracefully he
measures his role, his little test
of the universe, his solo blast.

Kiss me in my throat
and sense the birds tumble from
the weathervane as wind changes
and the smell of rain comes
with no rain, only lightning afar.
He's pleased with himself,
his flight from the scene
of himself with her on the sofa:
her legs in the air, her lips
about to bleed from being bitten.

Kiss me again, he whispers,
and she opens her eyes to the stranger,
to his small cold hands and his
smile hooked on like a toy piano.

Kiss me and I'll quickly alter
the rumours about you.
You've come a long way and still the music
slips your mind though you were
numbed by its beauty, its rhythm.

Enigma In C Minor

Yesterday I had a fever
thinking about you.
I burned whenever I conjured
your slanted smile.

You stood before me
fluttering the sleeves
of your blouse
like paper torches
your hard blue eyes
boring through me.

Later, you covered my mouth
with crushed mint
and poured cream on my head.

I'll wonder always
why you did this.

The Help Showed Disdain

A piano lightly showered the hot evening.

The red chair was mine.
The red parrot was not.

Everybody dined immaculately.
I was simply exhaust in the traffic
and the traffic surged through
stalled conversations
and other impediments.

Banter proclaimed of all things
the richness of their lives
flung about like ostrich feathers.
The hotel hung upon the sky
the women upon themselves
swaying under blue and purple petticoats
and choked in pearls that choked me
to watch.

The piano could have encouraged
them to prolong the dancing
taking on at last the ooze
of their liqueurs

all of them embracing in the moonlight later on
then retiring through the flowers
of a very humid night
not dismissed and flushed as I was.

A Small Complaint

Each day they come and take a little piece of me.
Today it was my ears. You're
not allowed to hear us anymore, you don't need them.
That's what they told me. Fine,
I didn't want to hear them anyway.
The week before they took my left arm
convinced I would be equalised.
They'd already taken my toes and my tongue
but I could still manoeuvre—and talking less
meant thinking more, so I am not depressed
about the tongue, though food tastes flat.
I'm afraid my eyes are next; yet one would
think they'd take the family jewels first.
But then again if they took those, they'd have
no reason to delete, destroy, and numb the rest of me.

Mannequin

Oh but we must try to bend the rubber tree so it
seems a wind of sea has blown it back.
Though with the sea I imagine rotting fish
and things, slimy wriggling things, and the burn
of salt on your lips when you're sunning in the sand.
Now, your brother's doing beautiful with
heads and hands, but what can he accomplish with the feet?
I find them much too long and much too pale
for my collection. Get them pedicured
or possibly remove them altogether. Give me air!
You are such a stumble-bum at times, I notice that you
need another shower. And why the turtleneck?
It's hardly cold today—your throat is sore?—so simple
yet so honest is your trademark. But please,
plant the tree, let's leave these broiling lights.
I like you but I also like the smell of living things.

Thinning Train of Summer

Elephants move into hiding, unchained
infants call out to their mothers.
Where are the mothers, where are they?

I dreamed of lions sleeping beside me
didn't know whether to run or not.
And when they awoke . . . and then

I dreamed of trumpet music, throbbing
muted trumpet music, pumping through
the vents, trembling the dream bed.

What's going on in the bedroom?
What is ever going on in the
bedroom, the airless, silent bedroom.

Palermo

The greenish light of an oil lamp tints the armoured knight
as some sublime event unfolds
for he watches attentively.

His sword has pierced the helmet of his foe.

Surprising he could stand so still,
perhaps a way of filling time.
But how can we be sure
of understanding such a man?
Pools of darkness lie behind him,
yet his eyes are pale beneath the hammered visor.

A child imitated a statue by a balustrade;
little angels clamoured above.
A priest clopped down a marble flight of steps.
That was more or less the situation.

The Zoo

1

Inside were the animals
jostling and you had
the whip
you snapped.

The animals' eyes turned away.

You kept the whip
above your head.
You meant business.
You weren't as funny
as the clown
they savaged earlier:
no hahas no
no hahas.

2

We should hand them umbrellas
and the stilts
we promised
or shovels for the elephants.

3

My sister provided the musical can
free of charge.

4

We shall once again
obtain our lighter forms
and filter over the beasts.

For now a ragged child
is tearing them apart with
no hahas no
no hahas.

The Weather Will Change

The cock knows the weather will change:
light extinguished early this evening,
restless dead leaves re-stirring in the wastes,
shutters tapped—he scarcely
sleeps through the long night
paralyzed on his perch,
the half-moon lost to him,
the dreaming hens so monstrous . . .

It soon begins to rain
and candlelight on tables in the house
becomes the shimmer of his pathway;
but it warms him only for a moment.
Afraid of falling into the void
he won't go anywhere at all
in this light with every wave
of his blood—yet morning arrives
like the pale lamb of God
and a black rooster whirls
in the window. Love calls.

For you the morning calls.

The Otter

Whatever happened to the fluid brain
behind the scenes, before clowning
became a way of securing sardines?
Make the shift to blue water,
take a little piece of the cheese
pitched by a child no bigger
than a mackerel, quick toss of
the all-smooth head—look at
the people by the pool, eyes
agog when he springs a new
acrobatic stunt. He's not fond
of the audience; on the other hand
he can take the applause. He can
eat the sardines until he feels
a need for a change. Then the
cheese is good, even the blue.

WHALE CONVECTION

Toot sinks low
arched back of sea:

rubber sailors plunge.
A ripple shows.

Open up the blue
a little better.

Crooked stems
glued to sheets

of afternoon blue:
"If you jump!"

Blue broke the fall,
hooks pierced the shell.

What about the crew?
Savage, savage.

"If you jump!"
I will be freed of this dream.

If you jump
you will fall from the sky.

If you jump
you will fall.

Distemper

Tumbling kittens upstairs
were creating a show down here
what with my full grown cat
getting sick about the action
he was missing, sick of me
his feeder, sick of my hands,
sick of my efforts, sick of
everything.

And yet the kittens pitter-pattering
reminded him that there were
others of his species
having fun, however
naively. What is this
for a cat, I thought, this existence?

What is this, thought the cat,
your existence?

The Transformation

Whenever things are left in their natural
simplicity, nothing has consequences.
The ball returns without
ceremony, the hair is matched
to the piece that had been shorn.
Thus, a complicated man finds it difficult
to put on his shoes one day.
So much as a toe will not enter them.
And yet the wedding feast
will wait for no man, not even
the gigantic barefoot groom.

He just wants to lie down in the field
beside the humming banquet hall
and take a deep sleep with his head
on a pillow of fresh carnations.
He'll do the fighting tomorrow,
but for now cuts the rope that
fastens him to this reality.
He puts away his scissors and does
another thing, he tosses the tiny shoes
into an illuminated ivy-tree.
Then he gathers the carnations and sleeps.

Take The Black Barge

Take the black barge
down the river of black liqueur.

Everyone else is gathering
in throngs in swarms.

The river of black liqueur
is wonderful to swim.

Ride the barge with me
swoon gladly on the bow side.

The world is having a bash
down the black river.

The world will have one last
brouhaha for the old times.

Black river climbs the skies
sweetly drowns the stars.

Sorrows washed away
in a black binge.

Unattributed

An insufferable correspondent
confirmed a difference of manners.
Meanwhile, single drops of water splashed my head.

"The iron has eaten into my flesh,
everything hums on a lower scale.
Little patches of snow
cheat me into happiness."

Overcome by anxiety and a fear
of losing face, my body
turned elastic as I fled the scene.

Yes, he could pass his life like that
in that tragic space he filled
forsaking lighter novelties.
His door was off its hinges.
"Obscure forebodings make any heart sick."
And so they should, my friend.

Chimpanzee

It wasn't the cap he was wearing, the fez-like red,
and it wasn't the strangled walk,
the ball-juggling, the grimacing.
A man with Aztec ancestors
encouraged the habit, offering
Marlboros. The ape received them
easily, not new to the conceit.
He crabbed backwards round the pavilion,
gathering an audience yet shunning it.

It was fuzzy that morning
but by noon the water swelled
with mystical bodies
and by evening yet others
danced as he went through the motions,
coughing a little, lacking the words to convince them.

Feelings of a Beast

Sometimes the order comes.
Sometimes days go by
before the door opens
and the light is lit, the bowl filled.

Whistling in the morning.
Whistling in the evening.

Sometimes it is the whistling
and the light going on
and the bowl filling up
and the light going off.

Not Insurmountable

A little coffee spilled on the sheets,
a German song on the radio
beating the yellow walls of the room.
I can pick and choose my warrants,
clap dead that moth insinuating
its powdery self—my only suit
full of holes—or step into the busy
schemata, comporting myself with haste.
That doesn't help, the potential reward,
nor would scalping my calico cat
for bawling needily in this
my hour of need, the bastard.
We've both lost our balls, though he
had no choice. The German song
concludes, the French announcer
mutters a few indiscernible phrases.
I long for understanding either way,
and not this heaviness. Yesterday
was much the same except for
the music, somehow lighter,
though black clouds jousted in the sky,
and the icy streets were dangerous.
Not forgetting that the sun is seething now,
I have a duty to propel my form
into the pool before the fulminations.

Red Hotel

Right off the cherry flat on the cream
and the light turning ahead
turning its soft spleen bottle.
Traffic and a black limousine
bleeding from left rear tire
body draped in white cashmere
bell-hop shining a beam.

I fear nothing don't you see
not the fire not the apples
rolling slowly to my feet.
I nod to fleeting strangers.
The juice cools my teeth
—it only lasts a while.

But then I hear the sirens
tearing out the heart of me
bolt from the radiant hydrant
make for the velvet lobby.

Costume Da Bagno

What spoils the harmony
of the bright clean day?
What carves and shades the being
displaced by splashing swimmers?

Sunlight lends its radiance
even as dark clouds encroach.

Bellowing ahead, a vast glittering arrival
triggers a complex chain of events.
Figures in the open fall away,
bloated inflatables lose their shape.

And then the beauty in the system:
the crashing blue light of your eyes.

Genius of Flora

The exotic is also familiar.
The entire scene composed of eight
brushstrokes—a park with wrinkled elephants
munching peanuts by its fountains, juxtaposing
fallen leaves all but the same flat gray . . .

And the dream is a soft gray rain touching
the dreamer. This one's at home nice and cozy
under goose-down and flannel, the park
miles away, the elephants diminishing.

In warmer light the head peels off harsh layers.
An island is unveiled: silken surf, perfumed breeze
and the vanity that nothing should be less than this.
It's warm again, all but summer again, the leaves so lithe
and green they laugh at more *intelligent* forms of life.

Here Comes The Tiger

Here comes the tiger.
I've seen him before and he's back.
Here he is, lunging and blazing.
Truth is, I'm not in the mood.

I'm not in the mood but
here comes the tiger
from God knows where
with his mad designs.

Here comes the tiger, the tiger
spreading his musky fire,
wondering why he inspires no awe.
Truth is, we're tired of tigers.

Holiday Of The Mind

No one wants to come here anymore.
Something's put them off, maybe
the dust, the galling mustiness,
maybe some other thing.
No calls returned—my fingers
ache from punching numbers.

What snakes our friends can be.
Yet I'll not die of loneliness.
I'll take a holiday of the mind
and what fun I'll have.
I'll put on a mental Panama hat,
festoon myself with flowers.
I'll think of pungent fruits,
a sky blue pool and palm trees.

The world has closed its heart to me
but I won't let this keep me down.
I'll sit in my bedroom
or in my living room
or in my bathroom
and beat my marimba.

The Book On The Jack-In-The-Box

1

I look to the end of the room
see the book over there
the one I want to read
before I sleep, the one
on the jack-in-the-box.

2

At this stage the party has ended
balloons go off piecemeal
ribbons descend like today
and it is tomorrow already.

SAM DIFALCO
lives and writes in Niagara Falls.